Engaged girl sketches

Emily Calvin Blake

Nabu Public Domain Reprints:

You are holding a reproduction of an original work published before 1923 that is in the public domain in the United States of America, and possibly other countries. You may freely copy and distribute this work as no entity (individual or corporate) has a copyright on the body of the work. This book may contain prior copyright references, and library stamps (as most of these works were scanned from library copies). These have been scanned and retained as part of the historical artifact.

This book may have occasional imperfections such as missing or blurred pages, poor pictures, errant marks, etc. that were either part of the original artifact, or were introduced by the scanning process. We believe this work is culturally important, and despite the imperfections, have elected to bring it back into print as part of our continuing commitment to the preservation of printed works worldwide. We appreciate your understanding of the imperfections in the preservation process, and hope you enjoy this valuable book.

ENGAGED GIRL SKETCHES

"*The girl gazed into the moonlit garden.*"

ENGAGED GIRL SKETCHES

BY

EMILY CALVIN BLAKE

CHICAGO
FORBES & COMPANY
1910

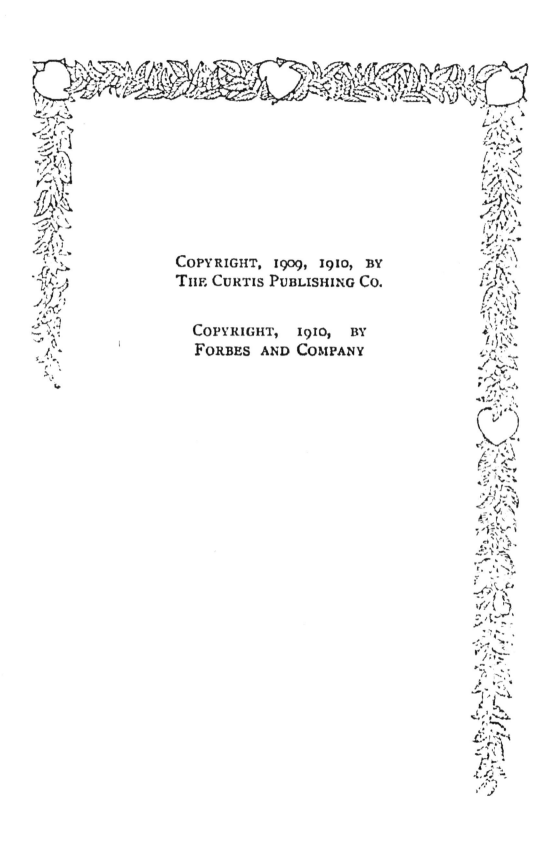

COPYRIGHT, 1909, 1910, BY
THE CURTIS PUBLISHING CO.

COPYRIGHT, 1910, BY
FORBES AND COMPANY

CONTENTS

	PAGE
An Obscure Situation	11
The Adorers of Anne	29
In the Face of Reality	51
A Dreamer of Dreams	75
When All is Fair	99
Moonlight and Roses	121
Qualities of Love	139

AN OBSCURE SITUATION

ENGAGED GIRL SKETCHES

AN OBSCURE SITUATION

"EUGENE is downstairs, as you suspect, Cecilia," observed Cecilia's younger sister; "but then he always is."

"Oh, not quite," laughed Cecilia, arranging her collar; "there, do I look all right, Mary?"

"You'll do," returned Mary with the insouciance of the younger sister. She paused for a moment. "Really, I wish you'd tell me when the wedding is to be. I want to begin at Mother to lower my dresses."

Cecilia only smiled again and went downstairs to the big living-room. Eugene Dysart, who rose to meet her, took her extended hand and looked into her eyes for a moment before speaking. When he did speak his voice was as warm as his glance.

"Your dress is very pretty, Cecilia," he said; "I like that white lace in the neck."

"Well, I am very glad," the girl returned, laughing, but not meeting his ardent eyes. "I did n't put on my hat. I did n't know the hour."

He drew out his watch. "It's just eight," he said; "I think we'd better start so we can be in good time."

A dozen young people had gathered at the home to which Cecilia and Dysart were going, and when the tardy couple appeared a sudden cessation of voices told Cecilia that she and Dysart had been objects of discussion. However, the gayety was soon resumed, but at the innuendoes directed good-naturedly toward her Cecilia's cheeks flushed until toward the end of the evening a tight, uncomfortable feeling bound her.

Either Dysart bore the laughing allusions with equanimity or he attached no personal meaning to them. Cecilia wondered which was the correct conclusion and blushed vividly at her own indelicacy for at once understanding. But later, when they were on their way home, Dysart made an observation which showed that he had understood the badinage:—
"Miss King seemed in rather a teasing mood tonight. You don't mind, do you, Cecilia?" he said.

Under cover of the dark the girl's lips trembled, for she had cared for the first time, but she answered lightly that she had not noticed anything different from the usual. Then, as she felt his helping hand, she tried to fling off her depressed mood. What mattered anything? And why should others busy themselves with her affairs? Did they owe the world the announcement that they loved each other? And, too, even if he should actually ask her to be his wife, she would wish to keep the beautiful knowledge to herself and have no disturbing word spoken. She dismissed an obstrusive thought and hugged again her repeated mental assertion that their understanding love required no formal ratification; that words were superfluous when eloquent eyes could speak. So when she parted from him at her door her face was radiant, and he, pressing her hand, gazed at her with an expression of yearning tenderness, though he spoke no word.

During the first months that she knew Dysart Cecilia's old friends tacitly left a free field for the newcomer, and at first, ignorant of the questioning eyes upon her, Cecilia went happily on her way. But as time passed she perforce became aware of the curious glances, and despite her in-

AN OBSCURE SITUATION

tense loyalty she wondered if Dysart guessed that she was subjected to annoyances that hurt her in proportion as she grew more sensitive. She watched him as he went imperturbably on, apparently indifferent or ignorant that she was suffering. But her trust in him she never lost, and while gradually his consistent silence became harder to bear she still told herself that the time of unspoken understanding was truly the most ideal of all periods.

One day she met an old friend, Nicholas Henderson, whom she had known since her childhood. He had settled in Arizona and Cecilia had not heard of his presence in her city. As he paused to speak with her his fine face expressed his pleasure at the meeting.

"Why, Miss Rogers!" he cried; "or may it still be 'Cecilia,' since I knew you when you were a toddler?"

"'Cecilia,' of course," she replied. "But when did you return?"

"A month ago. I did n't look you up — well, because I have been very busy —" he smiled his lame explanation at her, and Cecilia spoke hurriedly.

"Come to see us, almost any evening, won't you?"

He nodded and they parted; but he took advantage of her invitation within a few days. When his call was repeated many times Cecilia was treated to laughing jests from members of her family. Mary told her she had not expected such disloyalty.

"Judging from the brand of my own loyalty I thought perhaps yours was as pure," Mary taunted.

Cecilia was for the first time deeply annoyed at her sister. "Will you please explain just what you mean?" she asked in a sharp tone.

Mrs. Rogers was present. She spoke gently. "Cecilia," she said, "is n't it natural that we should be interested in you and your affairs? I shall be very glad to hear any confidence that you may want to give."

"But I have none to give," protested Cecilia, with a sudden, fierce rebellion rising within her.

"Then I don't understand at all," went on Mrs. Rogers. "When I was young—"

"Oh, please, Mother—I've heard so many of your reminiscences," Cecilia began, then shrank at the surprised pain in her mother's face. "I'm sorry," she said, quickly repentant. "But I cannot understand people's curiosity."

"I do not mean to be inquisitive, dear," said Mrs. Rogers, and her voice trembled, while Mary looked indignantly at her sister, "but Eugene has been coming here for more than a year, and you have accepted his attentions exclusively. So many friends have asked me if there is an engagement, and I have been sorry to say that you have told me nothing."

"Why should they ask?" cried Cecilia stormily. "Can't Eugene be simply a friend? Am I never to have any rest from questioning?"

But Mrs. Rogers lapsed into a hurt silence, and Cecilia, with no apology, left the room to seek solitude upstairs. She was filled with compunction at having so spoken to her mother, and with a strange terror at her heart she realized that a feeling of bitterness toward Dysart was creeping upon her: a feeling that he had subjected her to unwarranted injustice by placing her where she could not answer even her mother's loving questions. But she could find no solution for her perplexity, and her brow was still furrowed with thought when in the evening she greeted Henderson.

Cecilia yielded herself to the charm of his personality, for he was clever and interesting. She remembered that years before as a very young girl she had greatly admired him. Then he had gone away and Dysart had shortly filled her horizon. Now she was beginning to revel in Henderson's friendship and to feel a certain relief that she might indulge in candor of both look and language. However sweet she had thought the unspoken understanding between herself and Dysart, this open friendship seemed clear and beautiful in its sincerity.

But she was not prepared for Henderson's sudden change of laughing expression to one of deep seriousness. In a moment it seemed he had spoken words that placed them upon a different footing.

"Cecilia," he said, "I love you, and I want you to marry me if you can." He hastened on, determined not to notice the pallor that overspread her face at his words. "I should not have spoken had I known you were actually promised to another; yet, not knowing so, I take my chance; my love for you has steadily grown since first I knew you as a little girl."

Cecilia felt a strange longing, a longing that she might give to him that for which he so ardently pleaded, and the pitying tears rose to her eyes.

"I am very sorry," she faltered then, meeting his open gaze. "You cannot know how much I wish my answer might be as you desire."

He stood up then, and coming close to her gently took her hand in his. "I wouldn't cause you one pang if I could prevent it," he said gravely; "and I shall not let this defeat overwhelm me. You must believe that." He smiled at her, but she turned her head away, seeing beneath the smile that which he thought to hide: "Cecilia, I wish you all happiness in the world."

Long after he had gone and while she lay sleepless in bed she found herself wishing with all her strength that she were fickle; that she could bestow upon Henderson her love. For did the other give her the highest, truest love when he had not asked her to marry him?

"He knows — he knows —" she sobbed, letting down for the first time all her carefully-wrought barriers. "He must know what humiliations I have to bear; he is unfair, unkind." Then suddenly she believed she knew the truth and she gasped. "Why, he does not love me — I have mistaken his attentions," she whispered to the dark. "He wants only my companionship that others may not trespass; and then if ever he gets tired he has said nothing to incriminate himself!"

Her eyes burning with tears and her whole being wrought to a high tension she slipped from the bed and flung herself into a chair. It seemed that for hours she remained crouched in unhappy meditation before her conclusion was reached. As, she thought scornfully, she could not well ask Dysart his intentions, she would release him. Then again the satire of her position touched her: she could not give up that which did not belong to her. So, still tossing and doubting, she returned to bed only to lie awake till morning dawned.

In the evening when Dysart appeared Cecilia greeted him with a look that strove to be unconscious. But whatever her glance implied the young man guessed nothing. He looked playfully at her.

"Well, Henderson's not here tonight," he said. "I've been meeting him here a great deal lately."

"No," she replied in a flat voice. "He telephoned Father that he was returning to Arizona."

"That was a sudden decision, wasn't it?" he asked. Then looking into her face he spoke quickly. "Why, Cecilia, did he — he didn't dare —"

"Didn't dare?" Cecilia repeated with a mirthless laugh. "Didn't dare what?"

"To make love to you!" Dysart's face was white now.

At his words there rose before her a picture of her mother's eyes swimming in hurt tears; there rushed upon her the memory of all she had lately endured. And now he asked her whether another man had dared to profess frankly that he loved her — and dared to ask her in a straightforward way to be his wife. All her natural and lovely sweetness seemed to leave and to yield to a host of strange thoughts from which even in that fierce moment she shrank.

"Why should n't he make love to me?" she asked, the words seeming inane in her ears with the many emotions hammering within her.

"Why, did n't he guess — could n't he see —" he stammered, then suddenly grew silent at the passion in the girl's eyes.

"Guess — guess," she cried, "guess at

what? Why, he took his chances," she went on, unheeding the pain in his face. " He asked me to marry him, knowing that if I promised he would probably be irrevocably bound!"

He was at her side now, a new, strange purpose, a new consciousness lighting his face.

But Cecilia turned from him when he would have touched her hands. "Don't," she said, more calmly. "I ought to love you. They say that love is sanctified and strengthened by what we bear for its object; well, I've borne enough and I've done enough. I've hurt my mother and estranged my father; I've lost friends because I resented their questioning —"

"But they had no right to question —" he began.

"Oh, I've told myself that a hundred times," she said. "But they do, nevertheless, and it's hard on the girl —"

"Cecilia," he cried then, "I thought to

spare you, dear, believe me. But first let me tell you that I love you with all my heart, but that I thought it right not to bind you by any promises. My circumstances are not good; I've been waiting till they brightened before speaking to you; and if they did not brighten — why, then you were free."

"Circumstances!" she cried passionately. "I care nothing for them; why, I would wait for all time for you if I knew — if I knew —"

In overwhelming tenderness and deep remorse he put his arms about her, drawing her close to him, while utterly spent and sobbing she yielded to him. "I did not understand, Sweetheart," he cried; "I was blind. I should have known that we are not alone in the world. I don't ask you to care for me now, Cecilia. How can I, when through blindness I have caused you so much unhappiness? But — but — if you can trust me I'll make up to you in years to come, dear — I'll make up to you —"

Cecilia withdrew herself from his arms. She did not speak, while Dysart gazed at her with pleading eyes.

"Won't you give me a chance, Cecilia?" he begged then, his voice unsteady with emotion. "Won't you give me a chance to prove to you the depth of my love?"

Then suddenly like the breaking of an ice-bound brook, the girl felt the sun of her real nature warming and uplifting her. She put out her hands to him while a quick, lovely smile touched her lips:

"Can you love me, Eugene, after I have almost stolen your prerogative?" she asked.

"Stolen my prerogative?" he cried, his voice ringing. "You have stolen nothing but all my hopes and aspirations, my heart and soul; they belong to you, Cecilia." He paused for a moment, then his voice fell to a whisper: "Since my unthinking silence imposed so much sorrow upon you I wonder if you will come to me now — my wife!"

At his words the color rushed to her face, and when their lips met they lived their supreme moment.

THE ADORERS OF ANNE

THE ADORERS OF ANNE

IF Anne ever stopped to analyse her regard for Kenneth Roscoe she would have reduced it to a few words: that she liked him very much; in fact, she believed she loved him sufficiently to marry him at some very remote day.

She told him so one evening when at last after a week's endeavor, he found her for a moment alone. He rallied her upon her solitude as he gazed quizzically about the room.

"Not alone, Anne?"

"Yes, quite alone," she said; "strange to say, I've not had a caller tonight."

"Of course, I don't count," he replied quietly; then he looked reflectively at her as she reclined gracefully in her big chair. Her face was pale, but Roscoe knew that the lovely color would come and go as she talked and laughed; the alluring expression in her eyes, the slender whiteness of her throat, her whole sweet personality enthralled him. "How do you keep up the pace, Anne?" he asked as she turned her eyes from his speaking ones.

"Why, I love it," she said; "I love admiration and constant attention. Now, another girl wouldn't confess that, Kenneth, and probably I wouldn't to another man. But, really, you don't count."

She looked affectionately at him, and repeated her assertion: "No, you don't count in that way; I'm always my true self with you."

"But why, then, won't you marry me, Anne?"

"Because I'm not at all sure that I care for you enough." She leaned forward and gazed half-questioningly at him.

"And I couldn't be content with your attentions alone. It is exhilarating to think there are half a dozen men waiting to escort me to the theater, or dance attendance in some way. Have I fallen out in your esteem, Kenneth?" she asked anxiously.

"You know better," he answered. "Our estimates are rather different, that's all, dear. I would be satisfied with you alone; that would be happiness and exhilaration enough for me."

The girl rose impetuously from her chair. "I must have pulsing life," she cried; "that alone is the reality. I've seen other girls give it all up — the lights, the flowers, the admiration, and settle down to a humdrum existence. Oh, it isn't worth it."

Roscoe did not answer, but gazed steadily at her, till she spoke hurriedly.

"Don't look at me in that way, Kenneth." She paused. "I wish you would take my advice," she continued in a moment; "go and find some girl who would be satisfied to amble through life — who wants no thrills and excitement."

"Well, perhaps I may take your reiterated advice some day," he laughed pleasantly at her, but she, with a consciousness of her own power, believed that he would never seek another.

It was this same power she liked to feel she exerted over many of the men who waited upon her. And she loved it all, the exchange of ardent glances, the faint pressure of hands and the homage that daily was offered at her shrine.

"There's time enough to settle down," she told her indulgent aunt with whom she lived. "And really I don't believe that I ever want to see in one man the whole world."

And so she went merrily on her capricious way, the object of many flattering attentions, and known as the popular girl of her set, a title that pleased her greatly.

She attended a dancing party one night

with Kenneth Roscoe. As she left him at the door of the dressing-room she looked up for one fleeting second into his eyes.

"I'll see you intermittently during the evening, I suppose?" she laughed.

"You'll see me all the evening," he returned firmly.

When next he beheld her she had emerged from her rather somber cloak and stood revealed in the beauty of rose satin. Her hair was piled high in a soft, luxuriant coil and her eyes sought his in teasing willfulness.

She danced with him once at the beginning of the evening, then before he could make his way to her again her program had been almost filled by a number of her private followers.

"Yet I managed to save one more for you," she said, smiling at him as, for a moment, he confronted her. "Are n't you glad?"

His mood, rather a serious one now,

sat oddly upon him at the time and place, and Anne, with an annoyed feeling at his unwavering regard, leaned nearer to him.

"Try and look a little more cheerful, Kenneth," she cried with whimsical impatience. "There is no immediate danger that I shall elope with some one else, you know."

Then she drifted away, and the man saw her first in the arms of one cavalier and then another, the brilliant smiles of her eyes and lips never abating; the gay repartee for which she was famed evidently never ceasing, judging from the amused glances of her companions.

Later, stimulated by her evening of admiration, and having danced herself into a fever of excitement, she felt her annoyance returning at Roscoe's unresponsive mood as they went toward her home.

"Now," she said, when he stood with her at the door, "I know that something has been troubling you. Can you not bear to see me happy, so in love with life?"

"Anne, you quite wrong me, dear," he said gently. "I have tried to reach a definite conclusion, and before telling you I wished to be sure that I was right."

"Accurate and deliberate as ever," she said. Then, her annoyance slipping from her, she smiled radiantly at him. "Are you going to tell me tonight? If so, please hurry; I don't like to hold nocturnal conversations."

"Well, Anne, it is this: I believe it best that I see you less often. More and more I want you entirely for my own; perhaps it is not altogether a selfish desire, for I have confidence enough to believe that I would make you happy."

"You might," returned the girl; "but soon your love would descend to the prose of affectionate regard, and now everything is poetry. Don't you see, Kenneth?"

"I see your point, yes," he answered.

Then: "I seem to lend nothing to your happiness, Anne, nor even to your enjoyment. And as for your need of me, that may be counted as nil. Don't you agree with me that since I can't help longing for your love I'd better stay away?"

"That must be for you to decide, Kenneth," she said softly, and with a half-regretful word she left him.

That he did decide against his frequent visits she soon learned, for a week passed and she heard nothing from him. And that she rather missed him she reluctantly admitted to herself, but in the joy of conquests, new and old, she went contentedly on her way.

"Why," she asked her aunt one day — "Why can't a man be satisfied with a woman's friendship? And why should he want to draw her into a life where sooner or later everything becomes uninteresting; where love becomes somnolent, and one day is a copy of another?"

Her aunt, a fine elderly woman who had been Anne's real mother since the girl could remember, looked for a long moment into the uplifted, petulant eyes.

"Spiritless — uninteresting?" she repeated, then her eyes misted. "Perhaps you remember my life, when seemingly it consisted of makeshifts, of strictest economies, and of few spoken words that showed my struggles were valued?"

Anne spoke gently. "I remember," she said.

"You could not know then that a certain knowledge kept me brave and uplifted; nor look within and see my compensations. You saw only the surface."

Anne, remembering her aunt's passionate grief when she was left alone, was silent for a space.

Then: "I have seen so many lives after marriage apparently drab-colored and unromantic; lives that seemed all sunshine before;" she said. "It seems to me there might be inner compensations and a little outward sparkle, too."

But, despite her light philosophizing, Anne examined herself with unaccustomed sincerity, and was startled to find that her present unlovely mood was caused by a longing: a longing for the renewal of Roscoe's companionship, and a deep regret that he could not be content with mere friendship.

But now the winter was at hand with its promise of gayety at theater and ballroom, and because of her enchanting loveliness and high spirits Anne was eagerly sought.

She went one night to the theater with a man named Graham, who had been attentive to her for a year. He was a man of distinction, and she felt a degree of pride that he should so constantly seek her company.

But now when the curtain was down as she gayly talked and her companion comfortably listened, an unpleasant impression entered her mind. She was one source of diversion to him, and her vivacity and wit he was complacently absorbing, giving her indeed his interest, but contributing no adequate return for her mental exertions.

She conceded, however, that he was patiently gallant when later, cogitating her new thought, she appeared distrait; but a working truth had forced itself upon her, and she went on from point to point, until she beheld herself some years hence, neglected and alone, since she no longer was able to afford entertainment by sparkling animation.

But her keen sense of humor came to her aid and also a frank diagnosis; she thought disdainfully of her real trouble. She so missed Roscoe's tender devotion that she was becoming hypercritical regarding other men.

Her aunt and a visiting relative joined

the couple later and, as they all left the theater and sought the winter garden of a near-by restaurant, Anne recovered her spirits in part and seemed her old self.

"Talk to me now," she said to Graham, and if her words contained a reproach it passed him by; "I have been gay all evening." She turned to her aunt: "Is it not time now that I should be entertained?"

Graham, at this remark, began to shower her with unmeaning phrases; at least so they seemed to Anne in her peculiar mood. And she did not attempt to show appreciation of his adulation, for she still felt a soreness toward him for some indefinite sin of omission.

"But I have always enjoyed just this sort of thing," she said to herself, and then fell into a contemplative mood that took no notice of the rest of the party, till, aroused by a plaintive note in Graham's voice, she turned to meet his eyes, plainly surprised and a trifle bored.

She then tuned herself to concert pitch again, and shortly he was once more her interested, amused attendant.

Her aunt saw the flush in Anne's cheek; saw the light in her eyes and the tremble of her lips. So she rose soon, hoping that when Anne and she were at home the girl would yield her confidence.

But Anne sought retirement with closed heart; also she closed her eyes and mind upon a host of questions that confronted her, and so troubled was she that when she awoke she was surprised to find that morning's light dispelled in part her unwelcome thoughts.

"It was but the mood of a moment," she told herself, and tried to forget.

Still Roscoe was absent from her company of admirers, and even when Anne sent him an invitation to an evening affair given by her aunt he did not respond in person.

She watched until the evening had

nearly worn away, hoping to see him, but it was not until ten o'clock that her aunt told her he had telephoned that he was kept away; then Anne devoted herself with more than passing attention to the guests. But she had a numb feeling of living entirely on the outside of things.

Yet with a strange stirring of her heart she watched the girl whose engagement had recently been announced, and whose fiancé hovered about her, carefully shielding her by an inadequate silken shawl from possible drafts, his every look betokening a quiet reverence which the girl returned with glances of deep affection.

Anne, unable to cease her regard of the pair, was glad when a young man, with whom she had laughed and danced during the past few months, approached and took her to a secluded spot where she might rest. She had not known how tired she was until she sank into a big, comfortable chair and closed her eyes.

THE ADORERS OF ANNE

Then, remembering her companion, and as though impelled by his unspoken expectations, she roused herself and began to talk in her usual eager, impetuous manner.

She was entirely surprised a moment later to feel his hand close tightly upon hers, and then, before she could expostulate or withdraw, to feel his kiss upon her cheek.

"I cannot understand —" she murmured; then she stood up very straight and tall, and gazed at him, waiting for his words of explanation, her deep offense very plainly written upon her face.

"I could n't resist — really," he said. "Can you blame me? — you are so lovely —"

His light words and manner were significant of the unimportance he attached to the incident, and with burning indignation Anne left him, nor did she speak to him when, later, with the other guests he took his departure.

Then did she fling herself into the ready, patient arms of her aunt.

"What is it, dear?" that lady asked lovingly.

"I don't want to be simply a source of entertainment to the many," the girl cried bitterly; "and when I saw Alice Keppren receiving such reverence, such adoration —"

Her aunt stroked the bowed head. "But, dear," she said at last, "you have so many admirers —"

At the words Anne turned away, filled with shame at the memory of the indignity put upon her earlier in the evening. She tried to understand why the affront had been offered to her, for her conduct toward men had always been exemplary, even though she rejoiced when she added one more to her collection of admirers, and she had regarded them all as simple contributors to her amusement.

Amusement? She smiled scornfully as she thought of her erroneous impression, for it was she who had furnished the entertainment, if Graham's attitude was a criterion of the part she played in the lives of the others. Perhaps, and she winced at the thought, perhaps she was classed with the many girls ready to give liberally of their society and lighter emotions in return for flattering though unmeaning attentions.

Then only did she allow the desire she had been quenching before to assert itself, and now she yielded completely to it. She wanted the regard of one who would love and cherish her whether she scintillated brilliantly or fell silent and pensive.

She must always have loved him, she believed now, dwelling lingeringly on his tenderness and care for her. She remembered forgotten instances of his unceasing

thought. It never seemed to matter to him what her mood,— gay, grave or petulant,— his love was always manifest, surrounding, uplifting and sustaining her.

She was surprised now at the stirring of her heart as an apprehensive question intruded itself upon her. Did he after all still care in the old way for her? Perhaps her lightness and indifference had at last done their work, and his love had died.

Then she smiled, not because she felt her own power over him, but because she felt his love to be too deep a thing to rise and fall at the instance of her whimsical moods. He had always refused to take her at the value she placed upon herself, but had seen beneath the shallow surface to her real qualities of strength and fineness.

Her whole being now yearned for him, and she was about to ask her aunt to write to him on some pretext when her natural sincerity came to the surface, and she herself wrote simply and directly asking him to come to her; saying that she had missed him more than she had ever believed possible.

He came the next day, and, waiting for no preface, Anne went to him and put her hand in his.

"I want you, Kenneth," she said simply. "Do you still want me?"

All the tender yearning that had lain in his heart leaped to his eyes, and with it a reverence that made the girl's eyes fill with tears.

"Love is worth everything," she said at last. "I know now. That knowledge came in a mental flash one night a week ago."

He waited, regarding her with profound tenderness.

"I have been relishing husks and letting the realities slip," she said then.

"Does it mean, Anne," he said after

a long silence, " that at last you love me? "

" I think I have always loved you," she answered. " But the admiration of other men, the adulation, all have seemed so real, while it seemed a giving up of all that made life interesting to marry."

" But I'll show you, Anne, how great, how fine love can be," he cried. " The thought of you has ennobled me. I knew you to be a splendid woman to whom I could look for inspiration."

The girl raised her face, flushed with happiness and pride. " An inspiration — dear, I want to be that. I want to be all that you would have me. And to think —"

" What, dear? " he asked as she hesitated.

" To think I pushed your gift away from me so long; your gift of life and work together."

His hands tightened on hers.

" Are you sure, Anne — oh, I believe you are, but I want you to say it — sure that you can give up all the admiration of others and be content only with my abiding love?"

The girl raised her glowing face and regarded him with love-filled eyes.

"I want just you and love," she said. "Besides," she laughed to relieve her emotion, "it's too hard to entertain and amuse so many others."

But suddenly the laughter ceased as in a passion of deep love he drew her close within his arms and kissed her. That was the moment she really understood.

IN THE FACE OF REALITY

IN THE FACE OF REALITY

WHEN after an acquaintance of three months, Marjory became engaged, her married sister with whom she lived asked gently, but with plain directness: "Are you sure that you really love Wilton, dear?"

"Of course, I love him, Josephine," the girl answered quickly; "he is everything I could wish,— handsome, polished and clever."

"You have always accorded beauty in life first place," Josephine went on, not yet quite satisfied, and putting her hand softly on her sister's shoulder; "I really believe you have made an excellent choice; but I want you to be sure of your own feelings, that is all."

Marjory laughed: "How old-fash-

ENGAGED GIRL SKETCHES

ioned you are, Josephine," she said; "but you need not doubt me now, for I am at last truly and thrillingly in love. Does that satisfy you?"

Josephine looked wistfully into the roguish eyes. "Girls have made mistakes, dear. And I want you to be happy."

She stooped and kissed the rather petulant face lifted to hers, and left the room, leaving Marjory to prepare for her lover.

Marjory's thoughts, slightly disturbed by her sister's words and manner, raced on with her nimble fingers. Surely she thought as a lover, hers left nothing to be desired. He was a figure to attract immediate and flattering attention. His handsome face was strong in line and gave undoubted evidence of character. His eyes were always filled with tenderness and thought for her; and his every act was touched with chivalry.

Then as she pinned two lovely, purple

orchids on her breast just as the doorbell rang, her face dimpled into a smile, and she put from her the slight depression, deciding that Josephine, as always, was "narrow" in her ideas.

Wilton Howland waiting to receive her in the little room off the library put down his book as he heard the rustle of her skirts on the stairs and went to meet her.

He took her hands gently within his own. "You are sweeter than any flower, Marjory," he said, and stood gazing at her.

Marjory blushed divinely. "I'm glad you think so," she said. Then moving closer to him. "Take me out, Wilton. The evening and the moon are both beautiful."

"Throw a scarf over your head," he said, at once; "and we'll walk down to the lake."

Marjory ran upstairs again, returning in a moment with a light shawl. "You

ENGAGED GIRL SKETCHES

don't really think I need it this warm night," she said, pausing on the last step and looking into the eyes lovingly upturned to her. "But you like to see me wear it, that's all."

"Guilty," he smiled back at her. "Now, are you ready?"

"Yes," said Marjory. She called to Josephine, and in a moment joined Howland at the door.

They walked lingeringly along the moonlit streets, until they found themselves near the lake. They sought an old bench sunken in the sands and seated closely together they gazed off into the line of slender green that lay clearly marked against the sky line.

Howland spoke first, looking adoringly at the girl beside him:

"About a year ago I sat here by the lake, alone; the days were empty then. It is wonderful to me," his voice fell and he touched her hand gently; "to know

IN THE FACE OF REALITY

that all the years stretch before us and that we shall live them together."

Marjory spoke softly: "The happy, happy years," she said; "with you always to lean upon; you who are so handsome and so strong."

"I don't think the first, even if true, is anything of a virtue," he said, with a little smile.

Marjory smiled in return. "I think it's both true and a virtue," she said. She hesitated for a moment then continued half-shyly: "Josephine has been trying to discover whether or not I really love you. She is so much older than I that she rather takes a mother's place. But there can be no doubt of my love for you, Wilton," she finished earnestly, moving closer to him in a caressing way all her own.

Twilight had fallen and under cover of its friendliness, Howland raised the girl's hand to his lips, holding it for a long moment in his strong clasp; and Marjory, as often before, repeated to herself that, even with her many lofty ideals, in Howland she had not been destined to disenchantment; for he was all that she had ever dreamed a lover should be, and her visions had been of a man distinguished in appearance, clever of speech and with a magnetic personality that should challenge the admiring attention of all. And his wooing charmed her and completely satisfied her; for while it had been tempestuous, it had never lacked the essentials of fine chivalry — a true gallantry that rendered the man extremely attractive to romantic Marjory.

Soon, when daylight had quite faded, the young lovers returned to Marjory's home. The moon resplendent bathed all in her silvery light, and Howland took no more ardent delight in watching Marjory's face with the transfiguring glow upon it than did Marjory in gazing into his,

IN THE FACE OF REALITY

telling herself over and over that here was a lover of true worth — bearing all the gifts of the gods.

Josephine and her husband sat on the wide porch when the young pair returned. The older sister turned fond eyes upon Marjory when she sank down beside her.

"Tired, dear?" she asked, gently.

"No," Marjory answered; then her glance sought Howland and her brother-in-law talking together under the porch light.

"David is not very tall, is he?" she said, looking into Josephine's face with a little apologetic laugh; "Wilton seems head and shoulders above him," she concluded.

"Never mind, little sister, I quite understand your innuendo," said Josephine; "David is not handsome, I admit, nor is he courtly, your favorite word. But he is true and big, and in my eyes quite everything that is good."

ENGAGED GIRL SKETCHES

"Oh," returned Marjory, wonderingly; "but isn't it remarkable that you see all that in him?"

"When he is so homely?" said Josephine, not in the least hurt; "No, that is not remarkable; but it is remarkable that you have the effrontery to hint at such a thing." She leaned near and kissed Marjory softly; "Dear little beauty-loving sister," she exclaimed, "I'm glad your lover is all that you desire."

One night Howland told Marjory that he had to leave the city on an important business trip. "I shall be gone for two weeks," he said; "an eternity!"

But Marjory denied him, smiling. "We can write," she said, and always emotionally-guided her thoughts swung to the new sensation of for the first time receiving a letter from him. "And the days will soon pass," she added.

But after he had gone, she discovered

IN THE FACE OF REALITY

that life did seem rather flat. She watched eagerly for his first letter, and when it came, she read delightedly its every phrase, breathing his love for her. She answered at once, then waited in pleasurable anticipation for the next letter.

But a week passed and she heard nothing from him till one morning a formal missive arrived, written by the matron of a hospital to which Howland had been taken from his hotel, stating that he was ill and had been unable to write himself, although he was now gradually gaining a little strength.

Marjory sat for a moment with the letter held between listless fingers, enduring a pang of pity for Howland alone in a city hospital, divided by an ocean's span from all his relatives.

In a moment then impetuously her resolve was taken. She would go to him! Surely her place was now at his side, where she could help to nurse him to health again. Here she thought was a new and interesting element in her love story.

Josephine with helpful sympathy applauded the decision, and also made preparations to accompany Marjory, a sacrifice the latter hardly comprehended. So within a day, almost breathless, not realizing fully that she was really on the way to Howland, with Josephine, Marjory found herself on the train speeding to the distant city.

When she was settled in her place she gave herself up to dwelling with romantic expectations upon the approaching scene when Howland should first see her. He would, she knew, greet her as always with his perfect manner; illness could not change him, nor subdue his ardent glances. And she in turn would meet him softly, charmingly, perhaps a little shyly.

And pursuing her enticing plans, she concluded that during her attendance upon him, she would wear a soft white dress, sitting beside him with her hand in his, at times perhaps reading to him and lifting her eyes often to meet his adoring gaze. She indulged herself for hours in her, alluring dreams.

. . . .

Howland wasted with suffering, changed to a shadow of his former self by the sudden, keen illness that had seized him, gazed up into Marjory's face when with Josephine she stood by his bedside.

"It was good of you to come," he whispered.

"I shall be here every day," she replied; "and you will soon be well and able to return home with us."

He smiled wanly. Marjory's eyes accustomed now to the dimness of the room could see his sunken cheek and the straggling, uneven beard that lay upon it. The inertness of his hand falling from hers, and his great lassitude, touched some hidden string within her to painful vibration.

Of necessity the first visit was a short one; but the next day while Josephine went to the children's ward, Marjory found that some improvement had taken place in Howland's condition, and she was to be allowed to remain with him for an hour.

But better as he was, Howland still lay weak and unable to respond to the girl's seeking glances; and once, even while she was talking to him, he closed his eyes wearily. Then Marjory sat up very suddenly, while a little feeling of hurt wonder grew within her.

As the time passed and the patient steadily improved, Marjory was permitted to stay with him for a few hours each day; and though a nurse was in attendance, Marjory's relation to Howland was pleasantly recognized, and she was allowed to perform many acts of service for him.

But, much to her disappointment, there

IN THE FACE OF REALITY

seemed to occur no chance to assume the pretty role she had decided upon, and having seen nothing of illness, it greatly surprised her that the virile man she had known now required constant, prosaic attentions that meant the entire putting aside of self and the facing of stern realities.

These revelations of the sick-room proved a shock to her. And often as she gazed into Howland's worn face, she felt an impassioned desire for the return of the chivalrous man who had anticipated her every wish; the man who, in his normal condition of youth and health and good looks, had charmed and held her, but who now failed to touch her, except with pity.

She tried to put these thoughts from her, but they had sunk deep. She did not realize how deep till one day toward the close of a visit at the hospital, the nurse raised a shade, revealing Howland with his wan, unpoetic face; then unable to control herself, she turned away, murmuring some excuse and sought Josephine.

"Let us go home," Marjory said, and together they left the hospital.

Josephine glancing at her sister's face forebore to speak at first. Then as her breath came haltingly in an attempt to keep pace with Marjory's quick, nervous steps, she said gently: "What is the trouble, dear?"

Marjory paused in her hurried walk:

"Josephine," she said; "David has not been ill many times, has he?" She looked in a wistful way at her sister, as though waiting for words that would bring relief to her.

Josephine answered quietly, not noticing apparently the strange question: "Not often, I am thankful to say; he was ill for a short time after our marriage, but then it was a beautiful experience to me."

"Beautiful—" Marjory's eyes widened with astonishment.

"Beautiful;" Josephine repeated firmly. "He had been ill before our marriage, and much to my regret it was impossible for me to go to him then. But afterwards when he had an illness, it seemed wonderful and inspiring to me that I could nurse him, wait upon him and be with him every moment of the day and night; it was a blessed privilege. I believe I was happier then than at any time before. Later as the years passed that first feeling quieted, but now I love him just the same — ill or well." She finished, turning to gaze into Marjory's flushed face.

"Did David look — did he look as he does now when you were first married — I've forgotten?" Marjory stammered in her confusion.

Josephine smiled, quite understanding the question. "He was very homely when he was ill, a great deal more so than when he was well," she said; " and also he grew to be very peevish — a surface irritability. But that made no difference to me. I loved him, that was all. And, too, I had learned his fineness, his greatness of nature; and that is all that counts, you know."

Marjory then was silent. But new questions were struggling in her mind. Once she thought with startling clearness that the strongest part of her love had been for Howland's altogether attractive personality; she had not learned, nor even thought of his deeper qualities.

She soon lost all her old buoyancy of spirit, but clung to the hope that all would be well when Howland was fully recovered. When his hair had grown — her sense of humor did then prompt a smile — and when he became his old devoted, handsome self, then the romantic element with its accompanying thrill, would again manifest itself.

IN THE FACE OF REALITY

A woman with her flowing hair and pretty laces may appear interesting while convalescing from a blighting illness; a man, never. And Howland, to whom the attack had done its worst, appeared even less attractive when up and able to be about than when he had lain in bed. But he was entirely unconscious of the impression his close cropped head and sunken face made upon the girl he loved.

And soon, fight as Marjory did desperately to keep the truth from asserting itself, it did finally force itself upon her. She had never really loved him! If she had, nothing could have changed her, or so she believed now. But she had never even known the real man, and had succumbed to a mere emotional feeling for him founded entirely upon his personable characteristics; and when by illness he was bereft of his good looks and chivalrous manners, all that attracted her was gone.

Often now she thought of Josephine, loving David because he was David.

If only, she thought, she had not decided to play the part of nurse! Howland would have returned to her his old, handsome self and she would have married him and never awakened to the fact that her feeling for him was based on a purely material, perishable foundation.

She turned at last for comfort to Josephine; candidly confessing the entire truth. " And I wish, Josephine," she said at last, " that I had not come here, but had waited at home for Wilton's return and finally married him. Then, perhaps, I never should have known that I did n't truly love him."

" That might be so," said Josephine, " if marriage were made up of moonlight, thrills and tender glances; but there are realities to be met, trials and sacrifices to be endured. With true, uplifting love you could bear all these, and besides find big compensations, but not without real love, Marjory."

"Let us go home at once," Marjory said then, impetuously; "Wilton leaves the hospital today and does not need me anymore." Then at the surprise depicted in Josephine's face she went on hurriedly: "I can't see him again; how can I tell him I have made a mistake?"

"You're about to do something very unworthy," said Josephine more harshly than she had ever spoken to Marjory; "you have not found Wilton wanting in anything of importance; yet you are going to leave him here with no explanation. I am disappointed in you."

"What shall I do, then?" said Marjory, but she knew and impulsively answered her own question. "I will see him," she said, "and try to explain."

"That is the only course to follow," answered Josephine; and Marjory, confused and miserable, shrinking from what was ahead, tried before she saw Howland again to think of the easiest way to tell him of her mistake. But when he did call all methods were forgotten, and she found herself speaking hurriedly, jerkily, not able to look at him, knowing the hurt she was inflicting.

"Wilton," she commenced, "I have made a mistake in regard to you; it wouldn't be true to say I have made a mistake in you, because I don't know the real you; I never tried to find out. My feelings for you were not established on substantial grounds — how strange that sounds, just like Josephine — no, let me go on;" she cried as he attempted to speak, "this takes courage and I must not stop. But when you were ill in the hospital my attitude toward you changed. You seemed to me a different man; I didn't know you as you lay there gaunt and ill. If I had really loved you, you wouldn't have changed so to me, don't you see? Or if you had changed in outward appearance it would n't have mattered in the least. But, Wilton, it did matter — terribly, and I know that our engagement must end."

He made it easy for her by understanding at once. "If you were doing this for any other reason, Marjory, I might try to alter your decision. But I remember now so many things during our engagement that makes me see clearly your meaning. I know, little girl, that attractiveness means much to you. That night down by the lake — I thought of your words afterwards — you said I was handsome and strong — being handsome meant nothing to me — but I realized it meant nearly everything to you. Why, you must n't cry, Marjory —"

A rush of intense gratitude filled the girl for his tenderness. "You do not hate me then!" she cried.

"Hate you! Surely then you do not know me, Marjory." His eyes sought hers, and she looked away unable to bear their look of pain. She was filled with pity; for she knew she might have spared him had she looked deep enough into her own heart; but she had gone blindly on.

She could say no words now to help him and so she stood before him with tense fingers locked; then as the moments passed, she found herself wishing passionately that he was not such a stranger to her. But stripped temporarily of outward graces he appeared as one she had never known. Her eyes were as pain-filled now as his when she was able to raise them to his face. Then she moved nearer to him and held out her hand: "I shall never forget your generosity," she said. "Perhaps — understanding a little of the real you — may change — my feelings — in a measure. Be sure — that I shall be honest enough to send for you if that ever happens."

He took her offered hand gently within

his own, and looking into her uplifted, tearful eyes he seemed to find a promise, while his heart told him that should she ever send for him the future would be sweet and rich for them both.

And Marjory, with her hand in his, felt, too, that with the knowledge of essentials, life held perhaps deeper, more lasting joys than she had dreamed of.

Thus their parting was rimmed with hope.

A DREAMER OF DREAMS

A DREAMER OF DREAMS

"ALICE has come," said Alice's father as the doorbell pealed.

"Yes, she's here at last," responded the mother, going swiftly to the door.

In a moment Alice's merry laugh echoed through the house as lovingly she greeted her mother. "Home again!" she sang; and then seeing her father gazing at her with adoring eyes she went quickly to him and flung her arms about his neck.

After a moment he held her away from him, while he looked into her sparkling face. "Glad to be here?" he asked, a little wistfully; "Not spoiled by adulation and the display of wealth?"

She shook him playfully. "The same dear dad," she commented; "Why, there's no place in all the world like this."

Filled with the melody of her young voice, the old home awoke. The girl's animation was contagious, and her brother, a serious-minded student at the age where he glimpsed that he alone could save the world, laughed as he teased her: "Stephen's just haunted the house since you were away."

Alice smiled, quite unembarrassed. "Did you entertain him, Mother?" she asked, mischievously.

"As well as I could," Mrs. Kingsley replied; "Father and I took turns;" she paused for a moment. "I'm very fond of Stephen," she continued with a meaning look directed at her daughter; but Alice entirely unconscious, made some light answer and disappeared into her own room.

A little later in the day Alice's mother telephoned to many of the girl's young friends, and in the evening despite a sudden rain, they all flocked to the old house, so beloved was Alice for her sweet spirit and her joy of life: and, notwithstanding the fact that she had travelled a good part of the day, she was quite unwearied and cordially welcomed all.

The smile deepened in her eyes when close upon the arrival of the others, followed her old schoolmate, Stephen Maynard. But no conscious flush mounted her cheek; she gave him only the firm hand of friendship while laughingly she rallied him upon his allegiance to her mother.

The young man with reverent glance watched her as she moved among her friends. The rareness of her; the splendid qualities of her mind and soul flashed over him with a sense of humility. Could he hope to win her?

It seemed that always she had responded finely to his highest fancy. As a little girl her soft laughter entranced him, and her quick tears for another's mishap moved him deeply. And as in wholesome beauty

she had grown to womanhood, she seemed an inseparable part of his life.

He lingered when the guests had departed, and with a little smile at him Alice's mother left him alone with her daughter. She understood; for lately she had been made his confidante.

Alice settled herself near him upon the capacious lounge. Her hair soft and lovely lay above brown eyes that gazed mischievously into his.

"Well, Stephen," she began; "what have you been doing during my absence? Dancing attendance upon some fair lady?"

"No, my fair lady was not here," he answered, trying to speak lightly.

"You mean me, of course," laughed Alice, untouched; "you are very kind, Stephen, but you cannot impress me with your seriousness. I can't believe the little freckle-faced boy who once slapped me is now my devoted cavalier."

"I still think you deserved that slap,"

he replied, gravely; "for you willfully risked blood poison after I had warned you."

Alice was silent for a moment. "But fancy slapping a girl," she said; "you were n't very chivalrous. I don't think I can ever forgive that blow."

He smiled. "Blow? Now, Alice, you know there was no sting in that slap. And what chivalry can a freckle-faced boy of nine possess? I saw a way of punishing you and I did n't hesitate."

"Well," returned Alice; "it was rather radical action, but, after all, I don't altogether blame you."

Maynard rose and began to speak in a low voice: "I could never hurt you in any way, Alice; you must know that." His voice changed to a lighter tone. "How selfish I am," he exclaimed; "you were on the train for several hours today, entertained a dozen friends this evening, and now stay to entrance me with your presence when you are tired to death."

"Well, it's kind of you to see it," she replied, with malicious humor, while not suppressing a yawn. "Come again soon."

She flung the taunt at him, and smiling back at her, he left.

Very opportunely, however, Maynard was sent away on business by his firm. And much to her surprise, for the first time Alice discovered a great abyss that his absence made in her life. And when for a week she received no word from him, she felt indescribably neglected.

She was annoyed at herself because she so missed him; she did not run to the door as formerly at the postman's ring, and in every way she tried to keep the truth from asserting itself. Then finally she half-shyly admitted to herself that after all she was very fond of this old schoolmate.

One night she was engaged in rather listlessly reading a book when the doorbell rang. At the sound she sat up straight, the color dying her cheeks while her eyes filled with a radiant and expectant light.

"I'm in the library," she called as the maid went swiftly down the long hall. "Show any visitor in here, Elizabeth."

She knew even before the eager steps reached the library door that Maynard had returned. She rose to meet him, and her heart leapt as he gazed at her.

"Did you get my letter, Alice, saying that I would come tonight?" he asked.

"Letter — Stephen — I received no letter," she said, still flushed and with sparkling eyes. "I thought you had — forgotten — me —" Her voice faltered.

Maynard spoke quickly: "Forgotten you, Alice," he cried. Then he paused and eagerly searched her face. "Alice, can you try to love me; I've wanted you so, dear, wanted you so."

She looked up at him then with a little smile. "Try — try —" she murmured: "Why, Stephen, I've already learned."

Later when alone, Alice settled deep into her chair and tried to realize that she had given herself to another's keeping. It had all been so sudden, so unexpected that she could not marshal into order her scattered thoughts. But the memory of Maynard's tender words vibrated in her heart and she believed that now she knew the divine significance of life.

And to Maynard she was the meaning of all things. Her tenderness seemed to flame into being at his approach though she never gave freely of herself to him, a half-shy reserve seeming to enfold her. But as they sat together in the evenings, the girl close beside him, their new relation seemed too wonderful to the man to be true, so long had he loved her and so long had his love seemed unavailing.

It was only after some weeks had passed that Maynard began vaguely to feel that a hush had fallen upon Alice's bright spirits. A question stirred him. Had he failed her in any way? But he could not in justice accuse himself. Yet more and more she grew to be like a rose curling its petals, seeming to offer a direct withdrawal to those about her.

Maynard finally realized very plainly the change in her. He could not understand at first; then he thought she must be ill, so quiet, so shadowy to him had she become. But Alice was in a land where only ideals bloomed. And she trod fearfully since nothing was habitual or familiar. Only things transcendental seemed to possess worth, and when Maynard laughed and talked happily, she shrank from him, while a little wonder rooted in her mind. How could he descend from the heights to the practical ground of mirth and animation?

All this Maynard could not know, and as time passed and he still laughed and enjoyed himself, more and more Alice deprecated his human acceptance of their new relation. And at last to hide the hurt that grew within her, she adopted an impassive surface that Maynard could not penetrate.

He arrived one night with theater tickets. Alice sat with a piece of sewing clasped idly in her fingers. She greeted him with a pensive smile.

"Are n't you ready, dear?" he asked.

"Ready?" she repeated; then seeing the tickets which he held forth she started up with a look of regret. "I forgot all about the theater," she admitted; "Shall I have time to dress?"

He sensed her reluctance. "Perhaps you 'd rather stay at home, Alice?" he suggested.

She glanced quickly at him. "O Stephen, I would very much rather stay at home," she confessed; "it seems so quiet, so fitting here — and at the theater the music, the lights are so distracting —"

she broke off suddenly. "You understand, Stephen, don't you?"

He nodded, although he was really perplexed. "Shall we read or talk then?" he asked, taking her hand tenderly.

"Just talk to me," she said.

"Well, today," he began, plunging in,—"I met Robertson. He has come back here to live. He is an interesting chap, very entertaining. He told me a story that I thought quite clever. You'll laugh at it, too."

Alice gazed reproachfully at him. "A funny story," she said; "Why, Stephen, how can you?"

"I don't understand, Alice," he said, after a short pause given to reflection, "for you used to enjoy a good story. You were always smiling and happy." He sat up very straight. "And, dear, you seem so changed."

"Changed;" Alice repeated; "of course my entire life is different. Everything is

so wonderful now, touched by the sanctity of our love."

"Oh, of course," he answered, vaguely; "shall I read then to you, dear?"

She nodded, and picking up the book lying near, he began to read aloud though in the depths of his mind lurked a puzzling uneasiness.

And so they passed their evenings together, Maynard endeavoring to grasp just what was required of him; striving to quench any regret that the girl whose keen perceptions and charming responsiveness had claimed his admiration seemed now to have lost her wholesome sense of humor and to have become almost a stranger to him.

But strive as he might he could not understand the subtlety of her expectations, and when his mystified mind sometimes sought direct answers by plain questioning, the girl shrank from him, and soon there fell a muteness between them that was a signal of coming disaster.

Finally Alice folded away in her heart the grievous belief that Maynard possessed no real sentiment. That while upon the wings of her love, she could rise to wondrous heights, he must remain in the valley.

And Maynard with deep pain believed that Alice had mistaken herself and did not love him. Else how could she hold herself so aloof from him? But he exonerated her absolutely and sadly blamed himself that he was powerless to make her happy.

"Alice," he said, one night after a silence lasting for some moments, "can't you be quite frank with me?"

The girl looked up and meeting his eyes she spoke without thought, impetuously:

"Perhaps we have made a mistake, Stephen; is that, too, what you think?"

She had gone now quite beyond the

range of his comprehension, but he continued to question her:

"Can you explain things?" he asked again. "Wherein have I failed? I have tried so hard to be worthy of you. Perhaps if you could show me my mistakes, I might be able to remedy them."

"Because you can't understand now," she returned then; "there is really no chance of your ever understanding, is there?"

"Perhaps not," he said, and soon, as never before, they parted with no word, Maynard searching his heart for possible light.

Alice went wearily up the stairs after a time, and at the door of her own room she met her mother. Mrs. Kingsley's eyes questioned her and the girl spoke hurriedly. "Stephen left early tonight."

"What is the trouble, Alice?"

The girl, filled with conflicting emotions, answered the direct question with impulsive words. "I believe we have made a mistake, Mother. I have been discontented for a long time. Stephen has no real sentiment, I have discovered, and recently I have begun to doubt his love for me."

Her mother answered at once with a warmth of feeling that made her meaning sink deep into the girl's mind.

"No real sentiment!" she echoed; "I think, Alice, he has more real, vital sentiment than anyone you know."

Alice did not answer, but with a little gesture of weariness she pushed open the door, turning once almost reluctantly to receive her mother's kiss.

"Good-night, Mother," she said. Then: "I know you think only of my good."

She closed the door and sinking down upon her bed, her strained tension relaxed and she yielded to the tears that had been close to her eyes all evening. After a few moments, however, she recovered herself, and then came a realization of the banality of her recent quick confidence to her mother. She tried to dismiss the remembrance as she rose to bathe her eyes.

As she turned from her dresser, her glance darted upon a photograph pinned above the mirror. She lifted it down and took it beneath the light. It was an old school picture, a group of children in her class and at her right hand stood Stephen. How well she remembered the boyish face with its serious, never-wavering eyes.

As she gazed a flood of memories came to her. Just after the picture was taken an unhazardous fire had broken out in the school building, and the teacher in an endeavor to avert a panic had called immediately upon Stephen to help drill the children into order. He was always dependable.

Alice remembered now that his lips were firm, and his eyes held a light that calmed the excited little ones; and when they were all safely out in the school yard he had sought her and inquired in his quiet voice if she were all right; and had she been badly frightened?

She thought, too, of the time when he had slapped her; she had never ceased taunting him about that; she knew that she deserved his reprimand; for she had put her hand into a mass of rusty nails, regardless of his express advice not to do so. But she had rejoiced even then that she had aroused in one so reserved a quick emotion, however she was punished.

And it was because of his undisturbed poise that as a high school girl she had snubbed him, turning from him to those who indulged in spectacular deeds and words. Suddenly and quite irrelevantly now she thought of her cousin's husband, who was always knightly and chivalrous; who constantly offered his wife graceful compliments and delicate attentions. And

Alice once had voiced her admiration to her cousin:

"How attentive and romantic Richard is, Leila; you have been married three years and he is still treading the clouds with you."

Leila had smiled, recognizing the thoughts of an idealistic girl; then as though impelled, however disloyally, she answered:

"I'd rather have a strong arm to lean upon and feel true confidence than stumble on the unsure footing of the clouds."

Alice had pondered these words, but only now did they seem at all clear to her. And while she stood thinking, the telephone bell rang. Her heart leaped at the sound. Perhaps Stephen had called her up. She felt now that she wanted him more than at any time in her life.

But going swiftly into the hall, and picking up the receiver her hopes fell when a woman's voice answered her. It was

Leila, her cousin, the one of whom she had been thinking. The voice spoke softly: "Is that you, Alice? Oh, I'm glad I caught you at home. I have matinee tickets for tomorrow. Can you go with me?"

Alice hesitated a moment: Then: "What is the play, Leila?" she asked.

"Just an ordinary comic opera," Leila answered; "Richard got the tickets. It's simply one of those shows all tinsel and sparkle; there's no substance to it, no plot; just an amusing thing for a few hours. Can you go, Alice?"

"I think so," Alice answered; "I am not quite sure now; suppose I call you up tomorrow morning, Leila?"

"All right, that will do, Alice; good-night, dear."

"Good-night," Alice answered and hung up the receiver. She walked slowly back to her own room, but in her mind a phrase repeated itself; "All tinsel and sparkle"; the words struck fire leaving a new sense of values to take the place of the ideals she had cherished.

"Well, tinsel and sparkle have their place," she murmured half-defiantly.

But her opened mind insisted upon forcing new truths upon her. It told her now that she had valued the ideal as the whole of her relation with Maynard instead of a part, making her deeply resent his cheerful humanness and his interest in practical things.

"Well, here's the difference!" she said again, and smiled softly at the sound of her own voice; "Richard gives Leila the tinsel and the sparkle, while Stephen will be an anchor for me; I've been nothing but the silly little schoolgirl that he first knew."

She went swiftly down the hall again, in obedience to a resolution just formed, and paused before the telephone, when suddenly the downstairs doorbell rang sharply.

It was half after nine, but Alice knew with convincing prescience that Maynard had returned to her. She flew down the stairs and flung open the door, but her words of impetuous welcome died as she saw Maynard's face. It was set in such lines of pain as touched her heart till the tears were perilously close. She believed that she would never forget the expression of his wondering eyes.

"Oh," she murmured in an unsteady tone; "come in; I — I did not expect you."

He stepped into the dimly lit hall, closing the door softly. For a moment he did not speak, but stood gazing into the girl's lovely, changing face. Then:

"I had to return," he began; "I felt impelled to see you and tell you that I understand at last after much thought — when perhaps it is all too late. I know that a man is often silent when he should speak, and I want you to know all you have meant to me." He faltered, but recovered and went on; " I am not a poet, and so often I have had to search for words worthy to show you how rare a gift I held you —"

He stopped, for some new expression in her face made his heart beat fast with renewed hope.

Then with a sudden exaltation of spirit, Alice put out her hands to him in sweet abandon: "You not a poet, Stephen?" she denied, tenderly; "My ears were not attuned, dear, that's all." Then after a long silence she smiled a tender smile, yet her eyes held their old merry light. "I think, Stephen," she said softly, "that you will not need to waste any more theater tickets — I'm quite restored to my normal self again. Now we understand."

Maynard did not answer, but drew her to his heart, holding her in so tender, so yearning an embrace that Alice's face was touched with a shining radiance — and her heart thrilled with gratitude that at last her vision was clear.

WHEN ALL IS FAIR

WHEN ALL IS FAIR

LUCILLA'S sweet face glowed beneath the fervor of Bracefield's words. And when shyly she gave him the promise he craved, she felt a thrill of surprise that he could be so moved from his usual calm attitude.

He was a perfect lover, dwelling with tender words upon the beauty of her eyes and hair; surely no one had ever so intimately known the subtle charms of his beloved.

The faint curve of her eyebrows pleased him; the suppleness of her slender wrist allured his artist fancy. And the days flew by wonderful for Lucilla in their revelation of love until spring came with undue warmth.

Then the days found Lucilla inert and

pale, the descent of the sudden heat making her languorous, but she was her old, vivacious self in the cool evenings, ready with her accustomed charm to welcome Bracefield.

"I love you in white," he told her one evening; "I think every woman ought to be compelled to wear nothing but light colors."

"Think of the cleaners' bills," said Lucilla, smiling at him; "they would be tremendous."

"Some way should be found no matter what the cost," he replied; "I like you in white even though you do look a little paler."

"It is n't the dress," said Lucilla; "I 've been having headaches lately during the day; the warm weather has made me very uncomfortable. So Father wants me to visit his sister in the country."

"I 'm sorry—" Bracefield began; then

went on quickly; "but if it is for your good, Lucilla, you must go."

"Shall you miss me?" she asked, knowing that he would, but anticipating his glowing words.

"I shall miss you every minute," he responded fervently; "but now I want you to go and bring back some natural roses with you."

So Lucilla made her arrangements; but a short time before she was to leave, one of the sudden blinding headaches to which she was prone seized her. She remained in bed all day with her mother hovering solicitously near her. Not till evening did the pain leave and then Lucilla, though very weak, insisted upon dressing to meet Bracefield.

"He will be so disappointed, Mother, if he does not see me," she said; "he has to go away on a short business trip tomorrow and I shall be gone when he returns."

So a very pale, nervous girl went slowly downstairs, at eight o'clock, just after the doorbell rang. She had not attempted any of the little elaborations of her toilet and her dark hair was brushed plainly back from her brow. She paused in the doorway of the sitting room for a moment and Bracefield, turning at her step stood and gazed at her in deepening surprise. Then he spoke quickly: "How plainly your hair is dressed tonight, Lucilla; I like it very much better as you usually wear it."

Lucilla flushed and her lips trembled slightly: "I have not been well all day," she said, sinking into a chair, "and I did not wave my hair as usual."

In a moment he was contrite, showering her with delicate attentions and loving words. But Lucilla did not immediately respond. She felt hurt that he had not at once noticed her weakness and pallor. Then she resisted the mood as unworthy.

WHEN ALL IS FAIR

She had understood that men did not notice things as women did.

So at last she smiled at him and listened to his explanation of his business trip and what it might mean for them both. "If I get this man Temple interested in my proposition, Lucilla, then perhaps you will consent to a little earlier wedding?"

"Perhaps —" said Lucilla; "but, Harry, I don't care about the lovely home you want to give me; or the wonderful clothes — I want only you."

"You are a dear little girl," Bracefield replied; "but pretty clothes a woman should have, and an artistic home is a lovely setting for a bride."

"But — I should be satisfied in a little flat and do my own work — I love to bake and make salads —"

"And incidentally spoil your hands," said Bracefield, touching her soft fingers. "I want your hands always to be white and lovely, dear."

"And my hair always in curl," said Lucilla, looking thoughtfully at him, though she smiled.

"I'm sorry I was so cruel when you first came in," he said; "but your appearance startled me — you were so different, so changed."

The clock in the dining-room chimed, and Bracefield rose quickly; "I must be off, Lucilla," he said: "I've got to take an early train in the morning, and there are some things I must attend to tonight."

He took her into his arms and kissed her softly, while Lucilla clung to him. Their good-bye befitted an intended absence of years.

Two days later Lucilla was in the country with her aunt, Mrs. Eaton, and her Cousin Julia, the latter a young lady of enthusiastic temperament; just now it was tuned to highest pitch by the fact that in a manner she had become what she designated a village "cheerer."

"That's my own term," she informed Lucilla when they were together in the white bedroom that looked out upon a glowing garden; "I never did believe in the way some persons dispense charity, so I founded this name and inaugurated an original method."

"How very interesting!" commented Lucilla, when at some length Julia had discoursed upon her usual line of action. "May I go with you on some of your trips?"

"Oh, will you?" cried Julia, delighted, and her eyes wide and earnest gazed into Lucilla's interested ones; "There are so many old persons, you know, who like to have me visit them; and with the practical flannels I leave for them, I also give them delectable bits of gossip and reel off a few good jokes; and even if my stories are ancient, as Father claims, my listeners enjoy them."

"Well, I'll go with you tomorrow, if

I may," concluded Lucilla; "I'll try to contribute a mite."

So early the next morning the two girls set out, both carrying baskets. When they emerged from their first stopping place, Lucilla's eyes were bright and her enthusiasm ran as high as Julia's.

"How grateful they all are," she said; "I don't wonder you like to do this work, Julia. I'm going to bake a cream cake tomorrow for old Mrs. Johnson. She said she used to love cream cake, but has n't tasted any for years."

"And she'll appreciate that more than a flannel petticoat," said Julia; "even if she needs the petticoat more. I know," she finished sagely.

So the two girls with love and sincerity in their work, went about the village bringing cheer and happiness wherever they stopped. Lucilla was quietly happy in giving herself, and rejoiced that a certain understanding of human needs never failed her.

When after three weeks her visit drew to its close, she really felt a certain regret, but she cheered those who had learned to watch for her with the promise that at a later season she would return.

"Mother and the others will be so glad to hear of your work, Julia," she said on the last day. "And I envy you your opportunity. I'm going to come soon again, if I may."

"Come next month — if you have time," answered Julia, mischievously; "and meanwhile select a few persons at home who need a little cheering and give it to them."

The thought found immediate welcome in Lucilla's mind, and she counted the hours till, arrived at home, she sat at the big dining-room table and told her family of her experiences at Julia's home.

A silence greeted her story, but looking

around she saw her mother's eyes filled with tears, while her father patted her hand gently.

"I'm going to do some 'cheering' here, Mother," said the girl; "You do lots of it, I'm sure; take me with you some time."

Her mother smiled her fond approval, while the eldest brother put his arm about his sister's shoulder and said with a loving little hug: "Our Angel of Charity; don't get too good, Sis!"

"I'll try not to," said Lucilla, giving him a hug in return; then: "I've got to fly now and dress; Harry is coming tonight."

Her father gazed lovingly at her: "I like that little dress, Lucilla; you needn't run away and change it. We are going to lose you all too soon; give us as many moments as you can."

"Harry likes to see me in lacy white," said Lucilla; then with a little sigh she went to her father: "I'm glad you like me without any frills, Daddy," she said. Then she started; for the doorbell rang loudly. "There," she cried, "Harry has come; tell Ellen to never mind; I'll open the door."

She ran into the hall, and flung open the door. "Oh, you're early, Harry," she cried; "I'm so glad to see you."

His eyes travelled quickly over her little navy blue dress, plain and unadorned, before speaking. "I thought I'd come early, Lucilla," he said; "I have pleasant news."

"I'm very glad," she cried; "come into the den."

He followed her and sank into a big arm chair. "I'm a little tired," he said; "I just got in town this morning. My man is interested; that means everything."

"And you can go ahead with the business as you first thought," said Lucilla, pulling a chair close to his. "No wonder you are happy."

Then seeing his glance again cast at her plain dress, she spoke quickly: "I'm sorry I didn't have time to put on another more dressy gown, Harry; but I was telling Father and Mother about my experiences in the country with Julia. And Father likes this little dress; he calls me a Quaker whenever I wear it."

"I don't like Quakerish fashions," said Bracefield, rather shortly, and remained silent for a moment. Lucilla spoke softly.

"Julia is so interesting, Harry; I'm sure you will like her. She is doing some very interesting work in her village."

"Work? What kind of work?"

Then Lucilla told him quietly but still with deep feeling. At the thought of one touching incident the sudden tears rose to her eyes. She offered a little apology, looking into Bracefield's face.

"You see how selfish I've been; or rather unthinking. I've never come in contact with any hardship. Now I'm going to do a little cheering here."

Her face glowed lovely and pink while she gazed at him, waiting for the fond touch of his hand and his words of approval. But he did not respond,—only looked at her in a cold little manner; then a faint shadow of annoyance deepened in his eyes.

"I don't understand why you should get morbid," he said finally in a toneless voice that yet held reproof.

"Morbid?" she returned; "Why, Harry, I feel happy, really happy that there is a little something I may do to help others."

"Still it isn't necessary," he replied quickly; "I don't want you to do anything of that sort. Let someone with nothing to commend her in the way of beauty or charm go in for such work." He paused for a moment as he caught her bewildered look. "And, besides," he continued, striving to imbue his voice with tenderness, "I don't like to see you cry; a woman's first duty is to look pretty, and it's rather a shock to see one's ideal with red eyes and trembling lips."

"No matter what the cause?" she stammered.

"I don't believe anything is grave enough to make a woman forget to be charming," he said. As she did not reply, he went on, changing his annoyed tone to a coaxing one. "Come, little girl, get your hat and we'll take a walk; we'll go where there's light and cheeriness, and where you'll become your old entertaining self again."

But she did not move, only gazed straight before her with a perplexed little frown between her eyes.

"What's really the matter?" he said then, and now his displeasure could be plainly sensed; "I don't understand."

"No," she said, softly; "no, Harry, I

don't think you do." She rose then and held out her hand. "Since I am rather tired and so are you, won't you excuse me now?"

"Why, certainly." He assumed his debonair poise quickly. "I'll come to-morrow evening. I hope by that time you will have quite recovered your spirits."

When he had gone, she stood for a moment at the foot of the hall stairs. The family was in the dining-room and she could hear their happy care-free voices.

She longed to go to her mother; but she resisted her desire and returned to the room she had just left, seating herself in a far corner.

The revelation of Bracefield's indifference toward any experience of hers, hurt her; and the belief engendered thereby that he loved only her lighter self, deploring any pilgrimage into a beckoning realm of thought, deepened her eyes with wondering pain.

She remembered now that often quite plainly he had been bored when in a sober mood she had reflected on things outside his prescribed circle; then quickly she had driven herself into animation.

Her mind, despite her reluctance, raced on, always questioning. Could there ever be mutual understanding? Would he not be insistent in his demands for one side of her, intolerant of any show of feeling that might tend to make her less interesting to him?

Yet she, too, loved merriment and the joyous things of the world. Her heart spoke now. But clearly the answer came. Life could not be made up entirely of ephemeral emotions; and could she endure always to have the deeper qualities of her being misunderstood and deprecated?

Again her thoughts turned to his apathy at her story of Julia's loving work. All day she had glowed with the thought of his sympathy and he had commented upon her red eyes and lack of charm!

But perhaps — perhaps after marriage he would not care if at times she had her graver moments; he would learn to respond and they would have their times of serious communion together. And if shadows fell he would be there to comfort her, as she would comfort and sustain him always.

But his eyes rose before her, cold and annoyed, and she knew with compelling certainty that he could never be a sustaining presence to her; his very nature precluded that possibility.

Yet, now she thrilled at the memory of him as a perfect lover. Again she felt the fascination of his debonair personality, and recalled the flashes of humor with which he dismissed anything serious that threatened to disturb his natural atmosphere.

ENGAGED GIRL SKETCHES

The voices in the dining-room now rose in merry discussion and Lucilla heard amidst the laughter her mother's gentle tones. She knew by heart the responsive look that glowed in her father's eyes. And strangely now a chord of memory vibrated, bringing a vision of her mother, years before, emaciated and with shorn head, gazing at her husband while he whispered that she still was fair as a rose.

And Bracefield, thought Lucilla with a half sob, had regarded her with disillusioned eyes when after she had been ill all day he asked why she had not curled her hair, utterly blind to her physical weakness.

Wearily now she rose and went again into the hall, intending to seek her own room. As her foot touched the lower steps, the dining-room door opened and her father came forward. He saw her, and a tender smile parted his lips. So always he greeted his children with a smile and an understanding word that made them worship him.

He came softly to her.

"Going upstairs so early, Daughter?" he asked, and refrained at sight of her pain-filled eyes from asking any further questions.

She searched his face. "Did you love Mother," she asked, wholly irrelevant; "did you always love her when she was not all vivacity and sparkle?"

The question stirred him, and the words came hurriedly to his lips: —"Your mother, Lucilla, is your mother— I have never known her to be less than beautiful; she has a charm in every mood—"

"Oh, Father, I know—I know," she cried; then suddenly creeping into his extended arms, she said: "Just hold me tight, Father, just for a moment."

He strained her to him, while his heart leaped within him at sight of her distress.

After a moment she drew away from him, then kissing him softly, she went on up the stairs to her own room.

Later her brother passing her door, paused for a moment.

"Asleep, Sis?" he asked, softly.

She opened the door quickly. "No," she smiled at him, but her lips trembled slightly. "Would you mind mailing this letter for me, Bobby?" she asked.

"Of course," he replied, promptly, taking the envelope from her hand. Then he looked closer at her. "Anything wrong, Sis? Feel quite well?"

"Nothing wrong, Bobby," she replied; "Good-night, dear."

She closed the door and went to the window. "It will not distress him greatly," she whispered; "and I should wrong him not to release him when I know what the future would mean to both."

She looked up into the sky dark and blurred, but when the mist cleared from her eyes there was a star she had not seen before.

MOONLIGHT AND ROSES

MOONLIGHT AND ROSES

THE horse stopped knowingly before Estelle's door, and for a moment before alighting from the buggy the girl gazed into the moonlit garden of her father's home. Never before had it seemed so fair to her, and the man on the ground waiting to help her seemed also to be touched with the romantic mysticism of the summer night.

At the contact of his hand she felt a sudden rush of blinding emotion, and she gazed up into the strong, manly face, which she could see quite plainly in the brilliant moonlight. For a moment they stood silent, his hand still lightly holding hers; then Estelle felt her heart leap with a new joy as he tenderly said to her: "Estelle, I love you."

He drew her to him, and yielding to the wholly sweet impulse she found herself in his arms and felt his kisses falling upon her flushed cheek.

When she could speak her words came shyly: "I never dreamed that you should love me, Leonard — or — or that I cared."

He did not answer, but gazed at her as upon a dream suddenly changed to wonderful reality. Then they turned together and went down the garden path, his arm still about her — his face transfigured with the light of his new-found happiness.

At the door they paused, and he bent his head till he could catch her low words:

"Why, only an hour ago I stood here waiting for you," she murmured; "the night was so still and beautiful that it seemed something wonderful must come to me. And yet I didn't think of you, Leonard."

He smiled at her. "We never know

when friendship merges into love," he told her.

"But"— she breathed quickly —"how soon we learn; I love you now, and a while ago I knew nothing of love nor dreamed that such a wonderful thing could happen to me."

He drew her to him again, and then with a little sigh she turned away. "Good-night, now, Leonard," she said softly; "good-night and happy dreams."

She watched him go down the moonlit path; he seemed unreal to her — a stranger. But the smile still lingered on her lips as she opened the door and went quietly into the house.

Her sister-in-law, Margaret, opened the door of her bedroom and listened to the girl's light approach.

"Why, Estelle!" she exclaimed, as she saw the transfigured face of the girl radiant with a light she had never before seen there. Then as Estelle stood quite near to her she put her arms about the slim shoulders and drew her close within her loving clasp.

"Tell me — what has happened?"

"The most wonderful thing," Estelle replied softly. "Leonard and I love each other."

"You and Leonard!" responded Margaret in surprise. "Why, I had not known —"

"Nor I," returned Estelle quickly. She looked up into the strong, calm face: "Does it always come that way, Margaret — with a rush — with the touch of a hand —"

"Not always, dear," Margaret answered. "You know, Will and I — we waited —"

"I know, dear," Estelle interrupted gently, for now that Margaret was alone after two years of marriage and living in her husband's old home Estelle had learned to love her deeply, to understand in part her great sorrow, and to admire the strength of character which sustained her so steadfastly in affliction.

Margaret for a moment looked away from the clear young eyes, then, stooping suddenly, she kissed the questioning lips and said brightly:

"We all like Leonard — your father, grandmother and I. We had not suspected anything deeper than friendship, but now I suppose we must make up our minds to lose our little girl."

The words rang in Estelle's ears with a little sad echo long after she sought her bed and lay gazing out into the splendid world. She could see the stars in their bed of blue, and the shafts of silver light that the moon cast down filled her room with soft radiance; and soon in a maze of delight at the loveliness about her she lost the disquieting thought of home-leaving.

The whole night had been one of luxury and indulgence in dreams that merged into reality when Leonard's hand touched hers; she lived the moments over and over again until, enraptured, she fell asleep.

The month of June with its roses passed quickly, and Estelle knew many hours of joy. But in her quieter moments she turned always to Margaret. In times of reflection she seemed to find in her even greater understanding than in Leonard, for Margaret always responded sympathetically to every call upon her love.

"What shall I do without you when — when I go away?" Estelle asked her one day.

"You will have Leonard," Margaret told her. "And he will supply everything — companionship, tenderness, and understanding."

Estelle did not answer, but only sought and clung to Margaret's hand. "Sometimes," she said, answering Margaret's puzzled look —" sometimes I believe I need a weight of some kind to hold me down. It is all so beautiful, so wonderful — this new world."

Margaret was silent, looking gravely into Estelle's glowing eyes. Then: "It is wonderful, Estelle," she said; "and you may keep it so all your life."

"Of course," Estelle said, with the utmost confidence; "I intend to do so."

Margaret smiled at the tone. "You must remember, dear," she said, "there are a few duties which marriage brings that may not appear romantic."

But Estelle sprang away with a little cry of distaste: "I don't want to think of anything practical now, Margaret," she cried; then suddenly her eyes widened. "Why," she went on, "I don't even want to think of Leonard!"

Amazed by her own words, the girl gazed wide-eyed at Margaret. But later, as she went downstairs and out into a world of beauty, she forgot her momentary confusion and became again her own happy self.

The marriage was to be on Christmas Day, and with almost incredible rapidity the months flew by until September came with her rich, golden offerings.

Estelle, still wrapped in the wonders of the world she had stumbled upon — still, as her grandmother expressed it, " walking softly on clouds "— met Leonard one autumn afternoon on his way to her home.

" What's the matter, Leonard? " the girl asked. " You look strange."

" Nothing," he answered, and at sight of her his face cleared; " I want to take a long walk this afternoon, so I left the office early. I was going to call for you. Do you care to accompany me? "

She nodded, and they fell into step together. " Not quite so fast, Leonard," she cried after a little time; " I'm out of breath now."

He slackened his pace, and in silence

they went on. Soon they left the town and came to a long road leading into the country.

"Where are we going?" asked Estelle.

"Why — why —" He stopped for a moment to look at her with eyes wide and somber. "Estelle, I want to stop at the parsonage on the south road, where you and I can be married."

Estelle gasped in amazement. "Leonard!" she exclaimed when she could speak. "I don't understand."

"There is nothing to understand," he said; "simply, Estelle, that I want you to marry me now. There is no use waiting until Christmas."

"But I don't want to be married now," said Estelle. She looked up at him with a smile. "Does the time seem long until Christmas?"

"Yes," he said. The word was a murmur, but Estelle heard it. They had resumed their walk, and Estelle, with little panting sighs, tried to keep pace with Leonard's longer steps. Finally she stopped, her breath coming quickly.

"I think I shall have to rest, Leonard," she said; "I cannot walk so fast. I'm tired."

In a moment he was filled with contrition. "Sit here, Estelle," he said, drawing her to one side of the road where a fallen tree lay. He seated himself beside her.

"Can't you trust me, little girl?" he said, taking her hand in his and speaking very earnestly; "I think it best that we should marry now."

Estelle was silent for a moment. Then her words came very low, but very secure. "I could not think of it, Leonard. I should be quite willing to wait until Easter, or Christmas after next. I am quite content."

He regarded her strangely for a moment. Then, "Are you quite rested?" he asked, and stood up.

She grew a little pale. "Thank you, yes," she replied. "Shall we return?"

He nodded, and they traversed the same road again. Once or twice his swinging arm touched hers, but no stirring, delightful emotion filled her at the contact.

When they reached her home she paused and looked up at him. "I don't understand things at all, Leonard," she said gently. "Perhaps, when you come tonight, you will explain?"

But he did not answer, only looked at her with eyes strangely yearning, an expression that touched the girl with pity, and so she left him.

Margaret stood arranging linen in the old chest. She looked up and smiled as Estelle came toward her, pausing for a moment to watch the work.

"Margaret," said Estelle at last, "if

Mother were only alive — that I could go to her and tell her all!"

Before Margaret could answer Estelle walked on into the little den her brother had furnished before his marriage to Margaret. She looked about the familiar room, with its many pictures and gaudy draperies, with a feeling of strangeness, so greatly had she herself changed.

And so this was love — this strange unhappiness that filled her! She recalled the night she had given her heart into Leonard's keeping. How happy then she had been, and how filled with excitement all her days had been since that time. She went on from incident to incident marking her engagement, but it was an hour later, when Margaret sought her and the girl felt her loving arms about her, that she quite understood.

"Margaret," she said then, "Leonard does not love me, and I do not love him."

Margaret did not answer in words but

lovingly drew the trembling figure closer in her embrace.

"He wanted me to marry him this afternoon, and I believe now I know why," said Estelle. "Margaret!" she sat up quickly. "Suppose I had married him! You know, I never really thought of marriage. It seemed to me that things could go on just as they had been ever since we were engaged."

"Yes, dear, I understand," whispered Margaret. "You thought only of the things of love."

"Yes, just of the romance," said Estelle; "and I believe I thought more of the fact that Leonard could play the piano and that I could sing to his accompaniment than anything else. And yet —"

"Yes, dear."

"It seemed so real, Margaret — that night out there in the moonlight, and now I know it was but a moment of glamour, and we both wrongly thought our emotion love."

"Perhaps," said Margaret hopefully — "perhaps, after all, you are mistaken."

Estelle looked at her with a little reproach in her gaze. "You know better than that, dear," she said. "Why, I have never thought of Leonard as part of marriage." She smiled whimsically. "I have thought always of love and happiness, but never of Leonard."

"And yet he wanted to marry you to-day," said Margaret.

"Yes, for he also understands now, but he believes he must be honorable at any cost, and he wanted to bind himself quickly, thinking the rest would adjust itself. But I know now there could be no adjustment, and that honor does n't demand the fulfillment of mistaken vows."

"I 'm glad, Estelle, that that knowledge came now instead of after."

"So am I," said Estelle. She touched

Margaret's face lightly. "Fancy having a husband who really should be only a friend!"

But beneath her banter Estelle felt a hurt, and wondered if within her there was something that failed of appeal and response. But courageously she faced the situation, strengthened by her knowledge that love was the great and absolute essential, and that no counterfeit emotion would serve in its place to sustain and uplift; no counterfeit emotion but would be overstrained and inadequate in vivid moments of life, whether full of joy or weighted with sorrow.

When, later, she found Leonard waiting for her in the dining-room, from which her grandmother and father had made discreet exit, she went swiftly to him.

"I understand quite well, Leonard," she began, and as he rose quickly and stood before her she continued: "I have no blame for you, no more than you reserve for me. We are both mistaken, that's all."

"Estelle —" he cried, but she went on quickly.

"That is why you wanted to marry me today," she said, "is it not?"

He spoke now with the light of courage in his face.

"You are right, Estelle," he said. "I had the truth forced on me one day a few weeks ago — oh, no, there is no one else" — in answer to her questioning eyes — "but suddenly I knew absolutely that it was not love I bore you — only the deepest, most sincere friendship. I bitterly scorned myself, as you may know —"

"There was no need for that," she said gently. "I think many a man and woman mistake the glamour of the moment for the reality of love. You must not think harshly of yourself."

He took her hands gently within his own. "You are the best woman I know,

Estelle," he said; "and I believe that if we were married at once everything would eventually be right."

"I think not," she said decisively. "No marriage can be entirely happy where love is not a factor in it. Why, see how learned I am, Leonard! I never stopped to think before."

"You are the dearest —"

She silenced him with a little gesture. "Shall we be friends?" she asked. "And shall we make a compact?"

"Anything you like," he said eagerly.

"Let us be quite sure the next time," she said laughingly. Then at once she became grave. "We should be glad that we found out the truth before it was too late," she said. "A lifetime of real unhappiness or passive endurance would have been ours according to our natures. And all because the moon shone one beautiful summer night."

And very reverently he kissed her hand.

QUALITIES OF LOVE

QUALITIES OF LOVE

IT seemed to Virginia that never had there been a more prosaic courtship than hers. True, she told herself rather bitterly, that when a woman has reached the age of thirty-three she must not expect to live a startling romance.

Within the last few years she had grown tired of life passed entirely alone — life that seemed dull and commonplace beside the full lives of those about her. There had been a time when work, ambition and the care of others had drowned every other thought and she had believed herself content. But when first she knew David Stirling she had admired his quiet strength, his uniform courtesy, and in time she came to depend upon him. And when very quietly he asked her to marry him she consented.

The thought of his home awaiting her and his one child, a little girl of eight, brought to her a feeling of absolute content. She had not known how tired she was until rest was offered to her.

"I wonder if you will term me impatient," Stirling asked her one night, "if I should desire our marriage to take place very soon?"

She smiled at him, a smile which made her face lovely and very youthful. "Impatient?" she said. "Were you ever impatient?"

"You hide an innuendo there?" he said, returning her smile. "I am not so very aged."

"Forty," she responded quickly; "you were very careful to tell me everything a few weeks ago."

"Of course," he answered; "was that not right?"

"Oh, yes," she said quickly, subduing a thought that she would have been satisfied with the reiteration that he loved her and asked nothing of dry facts. "I think I can be ready to marry you in three months," she told him then.

"Very well," he answered gravely. "I have not told Loretta yet of our impending marriage."

Virginia gazed in a little fear at him. "Do you think she will welcome the thought?" she asked.

"She will become accustomed to it," he said. "She does not remember her mother, but I have told her a great deal about her and she tenderly cherishes her memory. Loretta is very dear to me, and I think you will learn to love her."

"How old is she?—I have forgotten," Virginia spoke in some confusion.

But Stirling did not notice her embarrassment. "Her mother died when she was three months old," he replied. "Loretta is now eight."

Virginia was silent then, and when Stirling had gone she still remained thinking. Once she gazed around the room, a faint distaste filling her for what she felt it lacked. It was a boarding-house parlor, containing the usual array of furniture designed for utility. It was beautifully clean and everything was in perfect order, but Virginia endured a sense of overwhelming loneliness, as often she had, before she promised to marry Stirling.

Early the next morning, before she left for the office where she spent her days, a dainty box of flowers came from Stirling. As a breath of fragrance reached her, a warm flush overspread her face. It was good to be cared for, and he knew that the perfume of his roses would lighten her working hours.

Another month passed rapidly, bringing the wedding day nearer. And when Virginia was not with Stirling in the evening she sewed the dainty things with which she was replenishing her wardrobe. And sometimes she hummed a little song. But beneath all she felt a vague questioning that stirred her uncomfortably.

One Sunday morning she walked with Stirling through the lovely spring park. She felt a warmth in her blood, a tingling of her veins that responded to the beauty of all Nature. She was young and glowing with life — and living her romance for the first time, she told herself shyly.

Then she looked at Stirling — at his strong, impassive face — and a cold hand clutched her heart. He seemed so content, immovable. She spoke quickly:

"It's rather great to be alive, isn't it?"

She had not meant to say just that, but now she looked up eagerly into his face, awaiting his answer. He did not speak at once. Then he said evenly:

"Yes; I am fond of the spring."

Virginia said nothing more. They retraced their steps, returning by way of his home, an imposing house that stood near the entrance to the park.

"Come in for a moment, Virginia," he urged; "my sister and Loretta will be glad to see you." He hesitated for a moment. "Loretta is very quaint; I think she will amuse you in a way," he finished rather proudly.

Virginia answered hurriedly. "No," she said with finality; "I want to go home now."

"Home!" he repeated, looking at her smilingly; "to that little room which you say looks out on a whitewashed court. I shall be glad when you leave it for good, Virginia."

"Oh, shall you, David?" Her question was a prayer, a cry for something she had missed.

"Yes," he answered; "I don't think a woman should be alone in that way."

The girl's heart sank at his level tones. "Don't come back with me," she said as he made a move to accompany her; "I'd rather go on alone."

Before he could reply she had left him, her tall figure in a moment quite lost to his strained vision.

Virginia hastened on to her own little room. Arrived there, she went quickly to the window, which the maid had closed and locked in her absence, and threw it open, drinking in the warm spring air. But in a moment she flung herself down in a miserable heap upon the lounge.

The lonely moments that she had endured here came back and pressed upon her; but those memories seemed to come in the form of temptation, and she thrust them from her. For now she quite yielded to the half-formed thought she had had for weeks. Stirling gave her only a lukewarm affection, and she must put from her the longing for a real home and the things of women.

At this decision she rebuked herself mercilessly; she held up to herself the dancing figures of her age. She was thirty-three, and yet could not be satisfied with the respect and the name that the man had offered to her. She felt within her the deep desire for romance — stirring, wonderful romance.

And she was jealous! She spared herself nothing now. Jealous of the mother of his child. Not, she redeemed herself in part, jealous in the ordinary way, but jealous that she could have only a measure of his liking. For of love he could not give her, since he could not be unfaithful to the memory of the woman he had first married.

She looked about the little room, with its pitiful makeshifts — its masquerading lounge, its screen that divulged rather than hid — and she shuddered with the fear that for long years she must still endure it all. It would be harder for her now, since she had believed a real home was soon to be hers; when she had thought herself quite content with the strength and reliance Stirling offered her. She had pondered, too, with a little timid joy on Loretta, who, perhaps, in her childish fashion resented the intrusion of a stranger.

Finally she rose and went to the small box behind the screen, where lovingly she had folded the articles she was working upon. She lifted a lace negligee, into whose dainty folds she had sewed many a thought of her bright future — with him.

But quickly she replaced the garment, as another temptation that leaped at her. She would not succumb, for eventually she would be miserable trying gracefully to accept the husks he offered her; and what, she asked herself — what meant the bare house that he called home, if he placed her therein simply as one to serve his com-

fort; where ever the memory of the woman he had truly loved must linger, and perhaps upbraid him with wide, reproachful dream eyes?

And so, with such thoughts for company, Virginia passed the day till, when Stirling came in the evening, she had quite resolved what course to take. Though she felt a hatred of her task she began hurriedly to tell him her decision.

He listened — quite unmoved, she told herself. And when she had finished he spoke as calmly as she had expected:

"You doubt my love — is that it, Virginia?"

"Not the quality of your regard," she evaded, for she could not tell him all her thoughts. "I think you are sincere, but, you see, I am not content with what you can give me."

"Have n't I made you understand that I care for you?" he persisted then.

"There's no use talking about it, is

QUALITIES OF LOVE

there?" she asked gently, and he sensed a certain finality in her tones that kept him silent.

She found herself alone shortly after, with a bewildered throbbing of her heart, and a bitter remembrance that he had taken her decision in a remarkably untouched way. And she raged at herself that despite his apparent indifference she cared for him. She had not known how much till all was at an end between them.

She recalled soon his grave mouth and tender eyes; yet they were not tender for her, but for her womanhood. And the best he had given to the first; and that was as it should be, Virginia repeated wearily; only, only, she wanted to reign in some heart where love and great tenderness should be hers — not a kind regard which in its way would always shield her, but which was but a counterfeit, after all, and entirely unsatisfying.

She went about her duties till, utterly

worn out, she sent word to the office one day that she would remain at home. She settled herself in her room in an attitude of listlessness, not knowing just how she would spend her time; she tried, after some time, to read; then, finding no power of concentration, she yielded to her depression.

It was nearly noon when she answered a timid knock at her door. Mary, the servant, stood smiling and behind her was a little girl.

"To see you, Miss Stanton," said Mary, and pushed the child into the room with a gentle hand.

For a moment Virginia gazed at the small visitor; then she knew that this must be Stirling's child.

"You are Loretta?" she said finally, and at the little one's nod Virginia took her hand.

"Did you come to visit me?" she said

softly, as she removed the white hat and slipped off the long coat.

"Yes," the child answered; then, gaining some confidence though her eyes were big and shy, she went on: " Father said you were at home alone; and when he's alone I comfort him. So he sent me to you."

So Stirling knew that she had remained at home. He was thoughtful and watchful even yet of her. Virginia sank into a chair and drew the little one close to her.

"I'm very glad you came to visit me," she said. " I have often wanted to see you."

The child did not reply, but smoothed her curls with an efficient hand.

" Betty was very cross this morning," she said; " so I did my own hair. When she is cross she pulls. And Auntie is away visiting; she nearly always is, though."

A chord vibrated in Virginia's heart at the child's innocent revelations, and stooping, she kissed the sweet face while the tears filled her eyes.

Then a thought came to her: here, surely, she was needed. But while it was a stimulating thought it carried no real happiness. She did not want alone to be needed; she craved love.

"Father told me about you," said the child, now leaning confidently against Virginia, "and I like you."

Virginia did not answer at once. "I'm so glad," she said; then, as the soft body nestled against her, a yearning rose within her to hold it in her arms.

"Are you too big a girl to sit on my knee?" she asked.

"Well, at night, when Father wants me to, I sit on his knee," Loretta answered; "but then, Father and I are chums. You know, I have no one but Father," she concluded.

Virginia, with a little cry, lifted the child to her knee, and in a moment the

QUALITIES OF LOVE

small arms were about her neck, the tender face lay against hers, and she felt a tide of pure joy rise within her.

"Father said," Loretta went on, " that perhaps you were coming to live with us; he said that before, but now he just sits and holds me tight. Have you done anything to him?"

"No," Virginia murmured, and with the child in her arms she seemed suddenly to be given a clearer vision. "But did you want me to come?"

"Yes," said Loretta. "I want everything that Father wants. He told me I must love you because he did; and I told him that I would give you a name."

"What name, dearest?"

"Othermother," said the little one in her gentle voice.

For a moment Virginia turned away her head; then she said in a low voice:

"And Father — what did he say?"

"He only held me close," Loretta replied, "just as you are doing now. Do you, too, like that name?"

"Very, very much," whispered Virginia; then, in a flame of understanding she closed her eyes. She had not fathomed the nature of his love.

"Father didn't go to the office today," the little informer went on; "he's in the park on our bench — that's where we always sit, you know. I'm going to him now. Will you come, too?"

"Yes," said Virginia; "you and I will go together."

In a short time they were walking toward the park, the small hand clinging tight to Virginia's. Virginia's heart was big with gratitude, for in the light of a little child's unquestioning faith she had found peace.

She felt a tender love that reached beyond the grave and touched Loretta's mother. She knew that always she would keep green that beloved memory in the little one's heart, and she would never disturb Stirling's reverence for the young wife who had left him years before.

For she knew now that love has its different qualities, and that Stirling's tender memory of his wife took nothing from the worth of his present offering. So all her doubts vanished as knowledge came, revealing the truth that love is great whether it be the ardent, romantic emotion of youth or the tender devotion of riper years.

As they entered the park Virginia saw Stirling through the trees, sitting dejectedly on the bench. Her love for him asserted itself as never before, and, still holding the little hand, she went quickly to him. As he saw her he rose, then stood waiting for her, a great question in his eyes.

"We have come, David," she said simply, when she stood quite close, and put her free hand into his quickly outstretched one.

"Virginia!" he breathed; and looking

at him then she wondered how she could ever have doubted his love.

"What a beautiful world!" cried the child, looking into the eyes of spring, and the hearts of her listeners fervently responded.

THE END

IN PRESS

By EMILY CALVIN BLAKE

THE SIX GREAT MOMENTS IN A WOMAN'S LIFE

A sane, wholesome message to women which appeared serially in the leading woman's magazine and there attracted such attention that there has been a great demand for its appearance in book form. The kind of a book that lives.

Cloth, 12mo, 75 cents

FORBES & COMPANY, Publishers
CHICAGO

CPSIA information can be obtained
at www.ICGtesting.com
Printed in the USA
LVHW060434290321
682798LV00012B/388